MW00365860

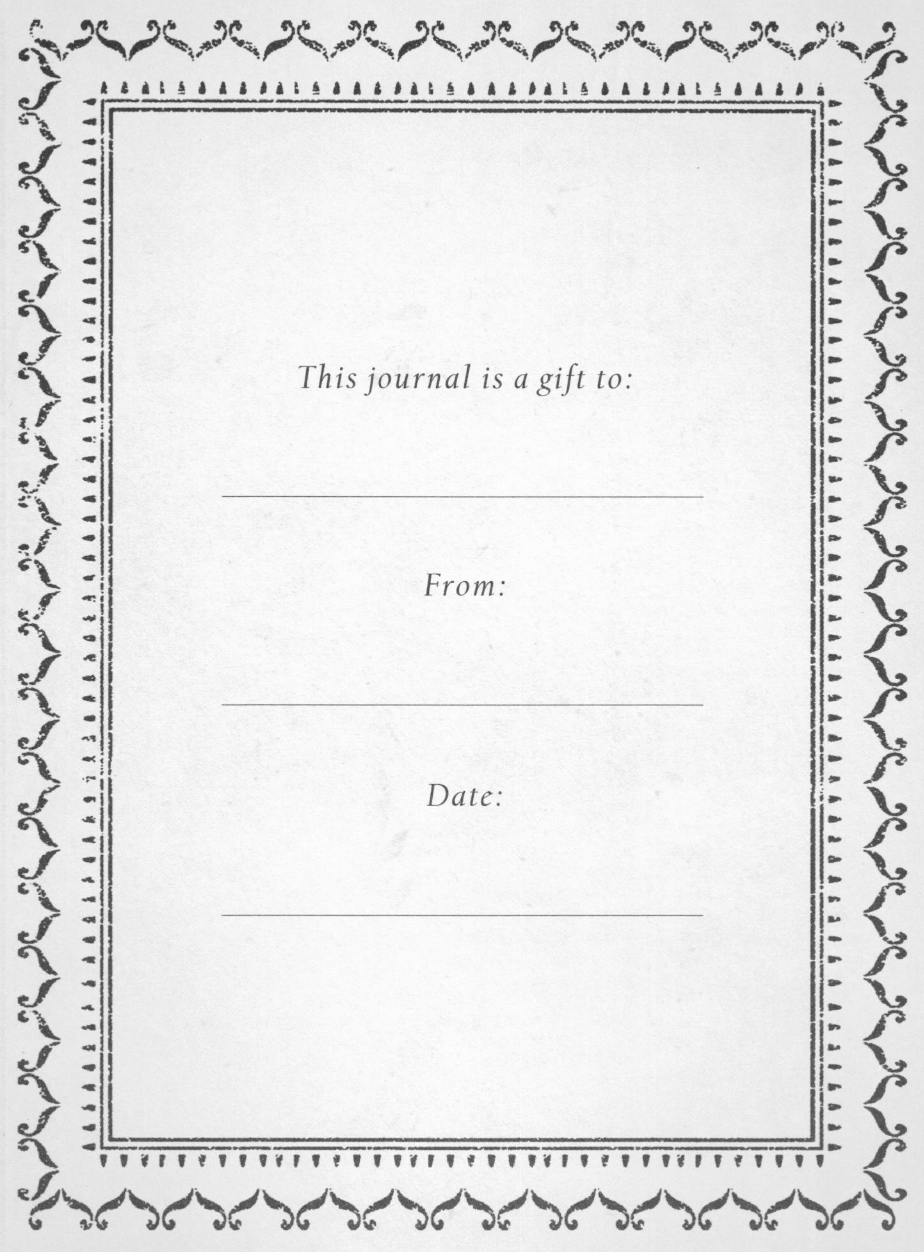

This journal is a gift to:

____

From:

____

Date:

____

Meet Me In the Meadow Devotional Journal

Christian Art Gifts Inc., IL, USA

Designed by Thinkpen Design LLC

Images used under license from Shutterstock.com

Printed in China

ISBN 978-1-4321-0182-4

12 13 14 15 16 17 18 19 20 21 – 10 9 8 7 6 5 4 3 2 1

Meet Me *in the* Meadow

ROY LESSIN

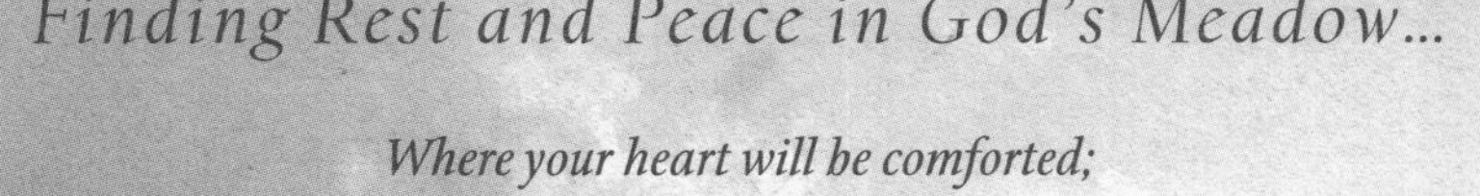

Finding Rest and Peace in God's Meadow…

Where your heart will be comforted;
Where your faith will be strengthened;
Where your soul will be renewed.

~ Roy Lessin

Into His Meadow

In your daily walk with Jesus, follow the Lord, your Good Shepherd, into His meadow—His dwelling place, His quiet place, His resting place, His protected place, His safe place, His nurturing place—where your heart will be comforted, where your love will be deepened, where your faith will be strengthened, where your soul will be renewed.

What things can you do today to find God's quiet and peace that bring you to His resting place?

My Prayer

The work of righteousness will be peace,
And the effect of righteousness, quietness and assurance forever.
My people will dwell in a peaceful habitation,
In secure dwellings, and in quiet resting places.

ISAIAH 32:17-18

Responding to God's Opportunities

Today God may give you the opportunity to manifest an attitude that reflects what He thinks and feels; to perform an action that expresses what He wants to do in a certain situation; to share words that speak His heart and His truth into someone's life; or to respond with a kindness that extends His grace and mercy to someone in need.

Today, how will you respond to the opportunities that God is presenting to you?

My Prayer

Let your light so shine before men, that they may see your good deeds, and glorify your Father who is in heaven.

MATTHEW 5:16 AMP

Leave Jesus?

Leave Jesus? Where else could we go?
We could never have a richer life;
We could never find a better way;
We could never know a deeper love;
We could never see a greater glory;
We could never belong to a surer kingdom;
We could never possess a nobler purpose;
We could never stand upon a firmer foundation;
We could never receive a fuller joy;
We could never hear a higher call;
We could never walk with a truer friend.

Why is it important for you to be close to Jesus' side?

My Prayer

From that time many of His disciples went back and walked with Him no more. Then Jesus said to the twelve, "Do you also want to go away?" But Simon Peter answered Him, "Lord, to whom shall we go? You have the words of eternal life."

JOHN 6:66-68

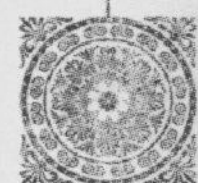

Inspected

Isn't it comforting and reassuring to know that the Holy Spirit can give us "the once over" before we head out the door to start the day. How wise we would be to daily let Him inspect us to be sure everything is in order—to be sure there is not resentment or bitterness hardening our hearts, to be sure there is no anxiety or worry weighing on our thoughts, and to be sure there is no unbelief or doubt clouding our spirits. How blessed our day would be if we could leave the house each morning knowing it is well with our souls.

How is your life blessed knowing that God has put everything in order for you?

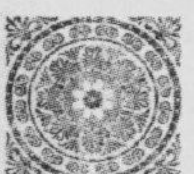

My Prayer

Search me, O God, and know my heart: try me, and know my thoughts: And see if there be any wicked way in me, and lead me in the way everlasting.

PSALMS 139:23-24 KJV

Blessings

A benediction of blessing:

"The Lord bless you, the Lord bless you and keep you! The Lord bless you in your youth and in your adult age! The Lord bless you in your basket and in your store! The Lord bless you in your work and in your home! The Lord bless you in your good times and in your worst of times! The Lord bless you in your comings and goings, from this time forth and for evermore!...And so may the Lord bless you!"
– AN ELDERLY SCOTTISH WOMAN (NAME UNKNOWN)

How are you blessed today?

My Prayer

The Lord bless you and keep you; the Lord make His face shine upon you, and be gracious to you; the Lord lift up His countenance upon you, and give you peace.

NUMBERS 6:24-26

Fear and Faith

Fear steals; faith rewards.
Fear questions and retreats; faith takes
what God has promised and moves forward.
Fear lets the inheritance we have in Christ go unclaimed;
faith takes hold of its possessions.
Fear quivers; faith fights.
Fear says, "later"; faith says, "now."
Fear is defeat; faith is victory.
Fear says, "You will be overcome"; faith says, "You are an overcomer."
Fear tears you down; faith moves you up.
Fear says, "how?"; faith says, "God!"

How do you let the strength of your faith overcome your fears?

My Prayer

*Look, the Lord your God has set the land before you; go up and possess it,
as the Lord God of your fathers has spoken to you; do not fear or be discouraged.*

DEUTERONOMY 1:21

Holiness and Glory

It is the Lord's glory and holiness (His majesty) that brings the fear of the Lord to our hearts. It is His glory and holiness that keeps us from an unholy familiarity toward God; it is His glory and holiness that keeps us from cavalier attitudes and actions toward the things of God; it is the glory and holiness of God that keeps us from becoming careless in our walk, careless in our speech, careless in our humor, and careless in our relationship toward God.

How does God's holiness keep you from being careless in your faith?

My Prayer

Holy, holy, holy is the Lord of hosts;
The whole earth is full of His glory!
ISAIAH 6:3

God Is, Was, and Will Be

Everything that God is today He has always been; everything that He has always been He will always be. Yesterday, God was there. Today, God is here. Tomorrow, God will be there.

Do you believe God is your provider all the time?

My Prayer

O God, renew us in Thy love today,
For our tomorrow we have not a care,
Who blessed our yesterday
Will meet us there.

– AMY CARMICHAEL

Heaven Is Better

It is good to walk the path of a pilgrim;
It is better to arrive at your glorious destination.
It is good to live the life of faith;
It is better to receive faith's final reward.
It is good to overcome and persevere;
It is better to wear the victor's crown.
It is good to live for Jesus day by day;
It is better to see Jesus face to face.

How are you preparing your life today for eternity in heaven?

My Prayer

Eye has not seen, nor ear heard, nor have entered into the heart of man the things which God has prepared for those who love Him.

1 CORINTHIANS 2:9

Quiet Hearts in Troubled Times

"God wants us to have quiet hearts, not troubled thoughts."

"We would never know the music of the harp if the strings were left untouched or enjoy the juice of the grape if it were not trodden in the wine-press. We would never discover the sweet perfume of cinnamon if it were not pressed and beaten or feel the warmth of fire if the coals were not utterly consumed. The wisdom and power of the great Workman are discovered by the trials through which His vessels of mercy are permitted to pass." – C. H. SPURGEON

How do you let God lead your heart when you face troubled thoughts?

My Prayer

Let not your heart be troubled;
you believe in God, believe also in Me.

JOHN 14:1

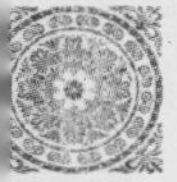

Truth

God is Truth

The Lord is the true God and the God of truth (the God Who is Truth). He is the living God and the everlasting King. JEREMIAH 10:10 AMP

Jesus is the Truth

Jesus said to him, I am the Way and the Truth and the Life; no one comes to the Father except by (through) Me. JOHN 14:6 AMP

The Holy Spirit is the Spirit of Truth

The Spirit of Truth, Whom the world cannot receive (welcome, take to its heart), because it does not see Him or know and recognize Him. But you know and recognize Him, for He lives with you [constantly] and will be in you. JOHN 14:17 AMP

The Word of God is Truth

Sanctify them [purify, consecrate, separate them for Yourself, make them holy] by the Truth; Your Word is Truth. JOHN 17:17 AMP

Are you allowing the truth of God to be the ultimate truth in your life?

My Prayer

You shall know the truth,
and the truth shall make you free.

JOHN 8:32

For His Glory

Each step is a right step when it follows His pathway.
Each word is a loving word when it comes from His heart.
Each touch is a healing touch when it is motivated by His compassion.
Each decision is a wise decision when it is made according to His will.
Each work is a good work when it is done for His glory.

How do you want your life to reflect His glory today?

My Prayer

For this reason we also, since the day we heard it, do not cease to pray for you, and to ask that you may be filled with the knowledge of His will in all wisdom and spiritual understanding; that you may walk worthy of the Lord, fully pleasing Him, being fruitful in every good work and increasing in the knowledge of God.

COLOSSIANS 1:9-10

Our True Guide

As we travel through life we don't need tips or well intended advice, we need a true Guide. We need a true Guide because we need to be guided. Sadly, many people seek guidance from guides who do not know the way and lead us to dead ends. God is the only true, trustworthy, fully qualified Guide there is who can rightly direct our steps and lead us in the way we should go. If we have the right Guide, we will know the right guidance.

Who is guiding your life today and what are you doing to ensure that God is your one true Guide?

My Prayer

Guide me in Your truth and teach me, for You are God my Savior, and my hope is in You all day long.

PSALMS 25:5 NIV

God's Guidance Settled in our Heart

For the believer, God's guidance is one of the greatest issues that must be settled in the heart. God's guidance is what separates the believer from the world. God is looking for those who want His way in their lives instead of their own way; His mind instead of their point of view; His wisdom instead of their strategy; His timing instead of their schedules; His steps instead of their shortcuts.

How are you separating worldly influences from godly guidance?

My Prayer

Whether you turn to the right or to the left, your ears will hear a voice behind you, saying, "This is the way; walk in it."

ISAIAH 30:21 NIV

Understanding God

Today, there is a great deal of confusion about who God is. We need to be wise and discerning. There are voices today that are telling us about a God they have created out of their own imagination. Some, in an attempt to make God relevant to our culture, have tried to pull Him down to our level of thinking and living. We need to see the Lord in clarity, in reality, and in truth. We need to see Him and worship Him in spirit and in truth. As we do, instead of having a theology that pulls God down, we will have one that truly lifts Him up.

Is what you believe based upon God's truth?

My Prayer

God gave Solomon wisdom and very great insight, and a breadth of understanding as measureless as the sand on the seashore.

1 KINGS 4:29 NIV

Brothers, I do not consider myself yet to have taken hold of it. But one thing I do: Forgetting what is behind and straining toward what is ahead, I press on toward the goal to win the prize for which God has called me heavenward in Christ Jesus.

PHILIPPIANS 3:13–14 NIV

God's Best to You

God can only give the best to you, because second best is not a part of His nature, His character, or His heart. If you cast yourself upon Him, He will not let you slip through His hands; if you drink from His fountain you will never taste of tainted waters; if you eat at His table you will never find stale bread; if you walk in His footsteps you will never be led into pathways of confusion.

What is God's best for you today?

My Prayer

Man finds it hard to get what he wants, because he does not want the best. God finds it hard to give, because He would give the best and man will not take it.

– GEORGE MACDONALD

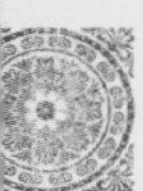

Our Savior from Sin

God sent His Son into the world to die upon a cross. He didn't die as a martyr, but as our Savior. He didn't die for a noble cause, but for our sins. Jesus Christ died to save us from every stain of sin, every shame of sin, and every pain of sin.

When Jesus shed His blood for our sins, God's justice was satisfied. The blood of Jesus Christ stands as the only redemptive price God will accept for the cleansing and forgiveness of our sins.

What is your response to Jesus today?

My Prayer

"Come now, and let us reason together," says the Lord, "though your sins are like scarlet, they shall be as white as snow; though they are red like crimson, they shall be as wool." ISAIAH 1:18

Beautiful Savior

Have your sins weighed you down? Let Jesus lift you up.
Have your sins broken your heart? Let Jesus heal you.
Have your sins had you bound? Let Jesus free you.
Have your sins condemned you? Let Jesus speak His words of forgiveness over your life.

Let Him embrace you in His arms of grace; let Him cover you with His mercy; let Him draw you close to His heart.

How do you intend to allow God to embrace you today?

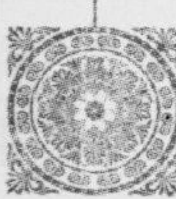

My Prayer

For as the heaven is high above the earth, so great is His mercy toward them that fear Him. As far as the east is from the west, so far hath He removed our transgressions from us. PSALMS 103:11-12 KJV

It Is Written

Life was never intended to be a gamble. "Chance" does not rule our universe; "luck" does not influence your existence; "fate" does not guide your destiny. God did not bring you into this world to live without a purpose, to exist without a reason, or function without meaning. You are not here because of chance. You are a unique creation of God. He loves you and cares about you. God desires to use you, according to His will, to make Him known to this generation.

Are you living with purpose today?

How are you making Him known to those around you?

My Prayer

David...served his own generation by the will of God. ACTS 13:36

Jesus Loves You

Jesus loves you, no one could be kinder;
He cares for you, no one could be more thoughtful;
He prays for you, no one could be more understanding;
He guides you, no one could more watchful;
He keeps you, no one could be more protective;
He blesses you, no one could more generous.

How do you desire to reflect God's love in your life today?

My Prayer

*That Christ may dwell in your hearts through faith; that you,
being rooted and grounded in love, may be able to comprehend
with all the saints what is the width and length and depth and height—
to know the love of Christ which passes knowledge; that you may
be filled with all the fullness of God.* EPHESIANS 3:17-19

God's Power Works Wonders

God is ALL powerful. When we hear about God's power we often think about wonders and miracles. These quickly get people's attention. His miraculous power can draw large crowds, cause people to travel long distances, and stir up great excitement. Wonders and miracles are manifestations of God's power that glorify Him, but they are not the only way God's power is revealed to us. There are many who will seek God for a new manifestation, but will not seek Him for a new disposition; for a new sign, but not for a new heart; for a new wonder, but not for a new life.

What are your motives for seeking a relationship with God today?

My Prayer

Now to Him who is able to do exceedingly abundantly above all that we ask or think, according to the power that works in us, to Him be glory.

EPHESIANS 3:20-21

God's Power Changes Us

We experience the power of God to change us when we are cleansed by the blood of Jesus Christ, when we take up our cross and embrace His will, when we are filled and controlled by the Holy Spirit, when we walk in obedience to His word, and when we trust Him with all our hearts.

What do you need to overcome today in order to experience God's power of change in your life?

My Prayer

That you may walk worthy of the Lord, fully pleasing Him, being fruitful in every good work and increasing in the knowledge of God; strengthened with all might, according to His glorious power, for all patience and longsuffering with joy; giving thanks to the Father who has qualified us to be partakers of the inheritance of the saints in the light. COLOSSIANS 1:10-12

God's Power Is Available to Us

People can be *touched* by the power of God without being *changed* by the power of God. As wonderful as it is to experience God's supernatural power through wonders and miracles, we must also trust in God's transforming power to live meaningful, victorious lives.

Each of us needs God's power to live a godly life, and thankfully, that power is available to us.

How do you recognize and apply God's divine power in your life?

My Prayer

According as His divine power hath given unto us all things that pertain unto life and godliness, through the knowledge of Him that hath called us to glory and virtue. 2 PETER 1:3 KJV

God's Care for You

Have you ever considered how much God cares for you? The following is a quote from Charles Spurgeon that gives us insight into God's care.

"Your sigh is able to move the heart of Jehovah. Your whisper can incline His ear to you. Your prayer can stay His hand, and your faith can move His arm. Do not think that God sits on high taking no account of you."
– CHARLES SPURGEON

How is God caring for you today? Can you reflect on the ways that He is blessing you, your family, and your friends?

My Prayer

The eyes of the Lord run to and fro throughout the whole earth,
to show Himself strong on behalf of those whose heart is loyal to Him.

2 CHRONICLES 16:9

New Day

Jesus gathered those He loved around an open fire in the early morning hours to share some breakfast together. He used this informal setting to reveal Himself to them after His resurrection. He reassured them in their uncertainty, and refreshed them in their weariness. He turned a difficult evening into a glorious new day.

Has God taken a difficult time for you and turned it into a new day?

My Prayer

Then, as soon as they had come to land, they saw a fire of coals there, and fish laid on it, and bread. Jesus said to them, "Bring some of the fish which you have just caught"... "Come and eat breakfast." JOHN 21:9-10, 12

God With Us

God is with us, in good times and bad times; easy times and hard times; gentle times and turbulent times. When we face difficulties, God will sometimes remove them, sometimes He will show us the way to avoid them, and other times He will show us the way through them. Having God's presence is more important than the circumstances we face or the people that are around us. When God tells you He will walk through something with you it means you have all you need—peace is there, strength is there, grace is there, love is there, because He is there.

Do you have God with you today? How is His presence helping you face today?

My Prayer

The Lord of hosts is with us. PSALMS 46:7

There's Something Different About You

In uncertain times you are secure; while others walk in fear, you walk by faith; in a world that is like sand, your feet stand upon a rock; with worry all around you, you have peace beyond understanding; in the midst of heaviness and discouragement, you have joy unspeakable; in troubled times, you have every comfort and consolation; while the world wonders what will happen next, you have hope strongly planted in your heart.

What makes you different and how is it helping to make a difference in your life and in the lives of others?

My Prayer

You are a chosen generation, a royal priesthood, a holy nation, His own special people, that you may proclaim the praises of Him who called you out of darkness into His marvelous light. 1 PETER 2:9

There's Something About You

Your heart has been toward the Lord, and His heart has been toward you...
You have taken care of the things that concern Him, and He has taken care of the things that concern you...
You have given Him all that is yours, and He has given you all that is His...
You have waited upon Him, and He will not disappoint you.
Your plans are now His purposes; your commitments are based on His leading;
Your desires fit into His design.
You have sought for His best and He has given you His highest.
You are someone special made in God's image.

How can you honor Him today?

My Prayer

May you be blessed by the Lord,
who made heaven and earth.

PSALMS 115:15

Anointing and Talent

When you are filled with self-confidence and achieve your goals, that is talent; when you are filled with the Holy Spirit and do the will of God, that is anointing.

Are you motivated by confidence, your own goals, or by allowing the Holy Spirit to lead your life?

My Prayer

Now He who establishes us with you
in Christ and has anointed us is God.

2 CORINTHIANS 1:21

God's Love Expressed through Us

Every attribute of God is an attribute of love.
Every expression of God is an expression of love.
Every word of God is a word of love.
Every gift of God is a gift of love.
Every motivation of God is a motivation of love.
Every choice of God is a choice of love.
Every response of God is a response of love.

What motivates you in how you express your love to God?

My Prayer

Beloved, let us love one another, for love is of God; and everyone who loves is born of God and knows God. He who does not love does not know God, for God is love. In this the love of God was manifested toward us, that God has sent His only begotten Son into the world, that we might live through Him. In this is love, not that we loved God, but that He loved us and sent His Son to be the propitiation for our sins. Beloved, if God so loved us, we also ought to love one another.

1 JOHN 4:7-11

Guide me in Your truth and teach me,
for You are God my Savior,
and my hope is in You all day long.
Psalms 25:5 NIV

The Attributes of Love

Righteousness is the character of love;
Holiness is the beauty of love;
Omnipotence is the power of love;
Omnipresence is the nearness of love;
Omniscience is the mind of love;
Judgment is the protection of love;
Grace is the favor of love.

How do you feel loved by God today?

My Prayer

We have known and believed the love that God has for us.
God is love, and he who abides in love abides in God, and God in him.

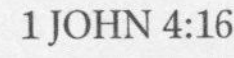
1 JOHN 4:16

Zero Tolerance

How much anxiety should you carry in your heart? How much worry should fill your mind? How much fear should agitate your soul? The best and only policy toward anxiety, worry, and fear is "zero tolerance". Through prayer, you must close the door to every enemy of God's peace. It is His peace within you that will stand guard against the things that want to trouble you and give you unrest.

What things are causing you unrest?

How can you rely on God to give you peace within?

My Prayer

*Be anxious for nothing, but in everything by prayer and supplication,
with thanksgiving, let your requests be made known to God;
and the peace of God, which surpasses all understanding,
will guard your hearts and minds through Christ Jesus.*

PHILIPPIANS 4:6-7

Your Work Matters

From God's point of view, whatever it is that you are doing is significant. God does not want any of us to struggle with insignificance. Your name may appear at the bottom of a work flow chart, or you may be at the low end of the pay scale, but that has nothing to do with significance. What you do, however big or small, is an assignment from the Lord and that makes it significant.

Is your work controlling you or are you allowing God to direct your work and its significance?

What are you thankful for in your work?

My Prayer

Whatever you do, do it heartily, as to the Lord and not to men, knowing that from the Lord you will receive the reward of the inheritance; for you serve the Lord Christ. COLOSSIANS 3:23-24

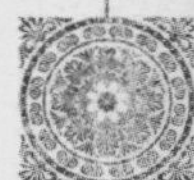

The "Perfect Peace" Ratio

How much peace does it take to balance fretting in our lives? The answer is that there is no "balancing point" for fret. We cannot balance something in our lives that is not to be there. God wants the peace/fret ratio in our lives to be

Peace = 100%
Fretting = 0%

Are you walking 100% in God's perfect peace today?

My Prayer

Do not fret—it only causes harm. PSALMS 37:8

His Kingdom within You

There are three things the Holy Spirit works within us to establish God's kingdom: righteousness, peace, and joy. It is the work of the Holy Spirit to produce all three. God does not want one-third of His kingdom established within us, or two-thirds, but the whole. The kingdom does not come within us in sections or on the installment plan.

How are you allowing the Holy Spirit to make the Kingdom known to those around you?

My Prayer

The kingdom of God is not eating and drinking,
but righteousness and peace and joy in the Holy Spirit.

ROMANS 14:17

Divine Guidance

It's good to remember that our choices are not based upon what is the easiest thing for us to do, or what is the most comfortable thing for us to do. Our choices are based upon what God asks us to do, not about the outcome.

What is God asking of you today?

My Prayer

We say—God intends me to be here because I am so useful. Jesus never estimated His life along the line of the greatest use. God puts His saints where they will glorify Him, and we are no judges at all of where that is. – OSWALD CHAMBERS

Rescued

A riptide is a strong surface flow of water returning seaward from near the shore. It can be extremely dangerous. There are spiritual riptides that can be a danger to our walk with Jesus Christ. Sometimes they can be subtle and go unseen, but once we are in their grip, they can pull us away from our peace, our joy, and our confident trust in the Lord.

What is holding you back from a closer relationship with the Lord?

My Prayer

This poor man cried out, and the Lord heard him,
and saved him out of all his troubles.

PSALMS 34:6

Casting Your Cares on Him

Perhaps this fishing analogy will help you take the steps needed to release all your cares to the Lord.

1. Get out your "fishing pole of faith".
2. Take all your cares and put the weight of them on a hook (the more the cares, the bigger the hook.)
3. Tie the hook to the line on your fishing pole.
4. Cast the line as far as you can into the sea of God's faithfulness.
5. Cut the line to make sure you don't reel back any of your cares.

Are you casting all your cares upon the Lord today?

My Prayer

Casting all your care upon Him, for He cares for you. 1 PETER 5:7

He Has Overcome the World

Your heart can be thankful today because:

God is in control;
He is on the throne;
He is wise and good;
He has made you complete in Him;
He knows His own;
He knows what He is doing;
He has your life in His hands;
He is working out His plan;
He has overcome the world!

What are you thankful for today knowing that God has overcome all things on your behalf?

My Prayer

I have told you these things, so that in Me you may have [perfect] peace and confidence. In the world you have tribulation and trials and distress and frustration; but be of good cheer [take courage; be confident, certain, undaunted]! For I have overcome the world. [I have deprived it of power to harm you and have conquered it for you.] JOHN 16:33 AMP

A Servant Leader

A servant leader is:

Someone who can set direction and inspire, instead of being bossy;
Someone who makes others successful, instead of using them for his advancement;
Someone who is genuine, instead of a manipulator;
Someone who motivates through encouragement, instead of through fear;
Someone who takes time to listen, instead of being set in his ways;
Someone who builds others up, instead of picking them apart;
Someone who creates loyalty, instead of mistrust;
Someone who imparts vision and unity, instead of confusion and dissension.

What does it mean for you to be a servant leader?

My Prayer

For even the Son of Man came not to be served but
to serve others and to give His life as a ransom for many.

MARK 10:45 NLT

When the Answer Is "No"

When we come to God with certain petitions, we can be eternally grateful that sometimes His answer is "no." It is important for us to understand that His "no" is not based upon our lack of sincerity, but upon the greatness of His wisdom. He is much too wise to say "yes" to any prayer that would bring us more harm than good if it were granted.

What is your response when you hear God saying "no" to you?

My Prayer

Now this is the confidence that we have in Him,
that if we ask anything according to His will, He hears us.
1 JOHN 5:14

Obedience Is Always Best

What is the best thing we can do as we follow the Lord? The answer is simple. The best thing we can do is what we have been asked to do. God does not want us to complicate things or put our own spin on it. Not doing what God asks us to do is disobedience, but adding something to what God has asked us to do is also disobedience. Let us walk with Him daily in simple trust and full obedience of faith.

Are you walking in obedience with God?

What steps will you take today in order to walk in obedience with Him?

My Prayer

Walk in obedience to all that the Lord your God has commanded you, so that you may live and prosper and prolong your days in the land that you will possess.

DEUTERONOMY 5:33 NIV

With and Without

With God, you may be broke, but you have the greatest riches; you may be single but you are not alone; you may walk through sorrow, but you have comfort; you may face difficulty, but you have hope; you may know your weakness, but you have strength; you may be unrecognizable to most people, but you are known by the Creator of the Universe.

As a believer, you are never out of God's sight. How are you acknowledging God in the moments of your day?

My Prayer

I am with you always. MATTHEW 28:20

Mercy, Peace, Love

It's a new day...you have never gone this way before. What you have planned for today is not what makes it meaningful. What makes it meaningful is that God is in it. He was in it when you first opened your eyes. He has sustained you through the years, greeted you with new mercies at morning's light, given you the breath of life, and promised to direct your steps until your journey is complete.

What have you planned for today that is meaningful because God is in it?

My Prayer

May you receive more and more of God's mercy, peace, and love. JUDE 1:2 NLT

Whatever He Says...Do It

When the Apostle Paul first met Jesus on the road to Damascus, he asked a very simple question; "What do You want me to do?" Paul spent the rest of his life doing what Jesus asked him to do.

His guidance will always lead you into His provision. As you do what He asks, you will find His grace to be sufficient, His strength to be abundant, His provision to be complete, His peace to be abiding, and His presence to be enough.

What is Jesus asking you to do?

How does He want you to spend this day?

My Prayer

Whatever He says to you, do it. JOHN 2:5

Seek the Lord while He may be found;
call on Him while He is near.

Isaiah 55:6 NIV

Joy Is Amazing

Joy is amazing and strength giving. Joy isn't just for the good times, but for the hard times as well. Jesus knew joy even while going through the agony and suffering of the cross. The joy that Jesus knew is the joy we need to know as we face every circumstance of life—hard or easy, bad or good, pleasant or difficult—and it is His joy that He gives to us.

Don't let anyone or anything rob you of God's joy today.

Are you seeking His amazing joy for your life?

My Prayer

Now may the God of hope fill you with joy. ROMANS 15:13

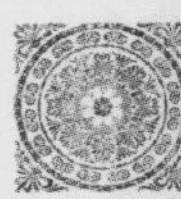

Secure and Certain

In the uncertain times in which we are living, God wants us to live as people of faith and not people of "sight". We are to be people who live amidst fear, yet have peace; people who live amidst sorrow, yet have joy; people who live amidst trouble, yet have comfort; people who live amidst uncertainties, yet have hope.

What can you do today to live in greater certainty—knowing that He has secured both today and your future?

My Prayer

Know this, that in the last days perilous times will come. 2 TIMOTHY 3:1

Rejoicing

Rejoicing in hope... A serving heart is a happy heart that is filled with the assurance of knowing that it is pleasing Him. A servant of the Lord can walk in fullness of joy because his confidence, expectations, and hope are in the Lord and not in man.

How are you rejoicing in the Lord today?

My Prayer

Let all those who take refuge and put their trust in You rejoice; let them ever sing and shout for joy, because You make a covering over them and defend them; let those also who love Your name be joyful in You and be in high spirits.

PSALMS 5:11 AMP

Faith

Your faith in God is your lifeline to His heartbeat; it is the hand that reaches up and takes hold of God's promises; it gathers in the spiritual treasures that are found in Christ; it stands upon what is sure and certain; it rests in what is unfailing; it says "yes" to every promise that has been written; it moves forward with all confidence in a God who cannot fail.

How can you strengthen your faith in Him today?

My Prayer

What is faith? It is the confident assurance that what we hope for is going to happen. It is the evidence of things we cannot yet see. So, you see, it is impossible to please God without faith. Anyone who wants to come to Him must believe that there is a God and that He rewards those who sincerely seek Him.

HEBREWS 11:1, 6 NLT

Our Response to God

I don't understand the thinking that says it's okay to be angry at God. It makes me wonder what people are angry about. God has never made a blunder, never made a mistake, and has never done anything wrong. There are no flaws in God's character. How could anyone be angry at someone who is perfect, who is all wise, who is love, who is altogether good, who is holy, who never sins, who never does evil, who never lies, and who has promised never to leave us or forsake us?

Have you ever been angry with life's circumstances, life's outcomes, or even at God?

What ended up being your response to Him?

My Prayer

To be angry at anything but what displeases God
is to displease God in being angry.
– WILLIAM BEVERIDGE (1637-1708)

Awe-inspiring

We must never lose the awe of God. To see Him is to carry a sense of wonder and dread, amazement and respect, worship and fear. The thought of coming into the presence of God should leave us speechless.

What amazes you about coming into the presence of God?

My Prayer

When Isaiah saw the Lord sitting on His throne (ISAIAH 6:1-5 NLT) he saw His holiness and cried, "Woe is me." When John saw the glory of the Lord (REVELATION 1:17 NLT) he fell at His feet like one who was dead.

Answered Prayer

Each of us should carry a thankful heart for every "yes" we receive from God as an answer to prayer. We can also be thankful He doesn't say "yes" to prayers that are not in agreement with His will—prayers that are based on our wisdom and not on His; that would bring leanness to our souls; that would put us in the wrong place; that would make us ineffective; that would bring us into wrong relationships; that would cause our hearts to cool; or that would keep us from His highest and rob us of His best.

What prayers has God answered for you recently? And were you thankful for His answer(s)?

My Prayer

I took my troubles to the Lord; I cried out to Him, and He answered my prayer.

PSALMS 120:1 NLT

Praise

The psalmist tells us to "Serve the Lord with gladness." "His praise shall continually be in our mouth." There is never a time when God is not worthy of praise. Nothing about Him ever changes, even in the midst of our most difficult days He is still faithful, still true, still on the throne, and still working out His plan.

What are you praising God for today?

My Prayer

In this you greatly rejoice, though now for a little while,
if need be, you have been grieved by various trials.

1 PETER 1:6

Skilled

It is important that you do your work well, but it is also important to be growing in your work and in your skills. Don't settle for "just getting by." Continue to find ways to grow, to expand your learning, and to improve your skills.

What are you doing today to not just get by but push your skills forward to grow, learn, and improve?

My Prayer

Do you see a man diligent and skillful
in his business? He will stand before kings.

PROVERBS 22:29 AMP

God Has Plans

Corrie ten Boom once said, "God doesn't have problems, He only has plans." God doesn't make bad days for you and good days for you. God makes each day fit perfectly into His plans for you.

Are you trying to plan your days or letting God fit His perfect plan for you?

My Prayer

A man's mind plans his way, but the Lord directs his steps and makes them sure.

PROVERBS 16:9 AMP

Peace Is not Based on Reason

Anxiety cannot abide in your heart when God's peace comes. It is a peace your reason cannot explain. You cannot "reason" peace into your heart. Peace comes because God gives it to you. Your circumstances may be anything but peaceful, yet His peace can abide within you.

Is there something you are anxious about?

If you are depressed, ask God to reveal the cause. Is it possible that the root cause is anxiety?

My Prayer

Anxiety in the heart of man causes depression. PROVERBS 12:25

The Financial World

As we experience the ups and downs of the financial world, many wonder what it all means and where we are going. The financial world, when the signs are bad, can bring confusion, bewilderment, fear, and panic to the hearts of people.

Are you giving your cares (including your financial concerns) over to God today?

My Prayer

Receive my instruction in preference to [striving for] silver, and knowledge rather than choice gold, for skillful and godly Wisdom is better than rubies or pearls, and all the things that may be desired are not to be compared to it.

PROVERBS 8:10-11 AMP

"I Am"

God used the burning bush to draw Moses aside, to hear God's voice and to discover how God wanted to use him. What Moses heard was God's plan, not Moses' plan. God does not come to us and ask, "What is it you would like to do with your life? Just let Me know and I will back you all the way." It is God's plan that we must follow.

Are you following God's plan or your plan for your life? What must you do (or change) in order to follow His plan?

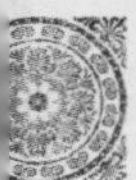

My Prayer

God replied to Moses, "I AM WHO I AM.
Say this to the people of Israel: I AM has sent me to you."
EXODUS 3:14 NLT

"I Am" Part 2

When God says "I Am" He is saying that He is all-in-all. He is your provider and He is your provision, whatever your need may be. In trouble, He is your peace; in lack, He is your sufficiency; in changing circumstances, He is your contentment; in difficulty, He is your joy; in weakness, He is your strength; in battle, He is your victory; in impossibilities, He is your miracle worker.

How are you relying on God as your "all in all?"

My Prayer

Jesus answered, "I tell you the truth,
before Abraham was even born, I AM!"
JOHN 8:58 NLT

Diligence

In the apprenticeship system, young people grew up learning a trade and learning how to work with their hands. Children who grew up on farms often learned that playtime was a privilege, not a right. Everyone who has a job has a choice to make. He can either be slack in his work or diligent. Employers notice the difference and reward those whose work is honest and noble.

How are you being diligent in your work time, your choices, and in your life?

My Prayer

He becomes poor who works with a slack
and idle hand, but the hand of the diligent makes rich.

PROVERBS 10:4 AMP

God, who has called you into fellowship with His Son Jesus Christ our Lord, is faithful.

1 Corinthians 1:9 NIV

What's It All About?

It's about the painting, not the frame; it's about the treasure, not the vessel; it's about His truth, not our opinions; it's about His glory, not our looks; it's about His love, not our niceness; it's about His purpose, not our plans; it's about His kingdom, not our agenda; it's about His reign, not our rights; it's about His life, not our efforts. It's about Jesus!

How do you define what it's all about in your life?

My Prayer

But we all, with unveiled face, beholding as in a mirror the glory of the Lord, are being transformed into the same image from glory to glory, just as by the Spirit of the Lord. 2 CORINTHIANS 3:18

It's Good to Wait upon His Promises

If you find that you are anxious about something ask yourself if you have prayed about it, and fully committed it to the Lord.

If you have prayed about it, committed it to the Lord, and are still anxious, begin to thank God in your heart and in your prayers for being in control of the situation. Prayer, commitment, and thanksgiving open the door to peace as you wait for His answer.

How are you being patient and waiting to hear from the Holy Spirit before acting?

My Prayer

The peace of God, which surpasses all understanding,
will guard your hearts and minds through Christ Jesus.

PHILIPPIANS 4:7

Wholeness

God wants you to be whole, in body, in soul, and in spirit. He wants you to be fully complete in Him, without any gaps, holes, or empty places in your heart. He who fills all, wants to fill all of you, with all He has to give.

What are the empty holes in your heart today?

My Prayer

And the very God of peace sanctify you wholly; and I pray God your whole spirit and soul and body be preserved blameless unto the coming of our Lord Jesus Christ. 1 THESSALONIANS 5:23 KJV

Health

Healing is a blessing from God and so is good health. In so many ways, God expresses His grace and mercies to us, touching us in our need time and time again—He renews your strength, restores your well-being, revives your heart, refreshes your spirit, and relaxes your nerves.

How has God blessed your life with healing and good health?

My Prayer

Beloved, I wish above all things that thou mayest prosper and be in health, even as thy soul prospereth.

3 JOHN 1:2 KJV

More Than Enough

The resources of God that He sends on your behalf are more than enough to bring you through each day triumphantly. If one angel is not enough, God will send two. If two are not enough, God will send ten thousand.

How has God's grace blessed you with more than enough?

My Prayer

The chariots of God are twenty thousand, even thousands of thousands: the Lord is among them as in Sinai, in the Holy Place.

PSALMS 68:17

You Are Not...

You are not alone—
For God is with you.
You are not defenseless—
For God is your protector.
You are not inadequate—
For God is your sufficiency.
You are not useless—
For God has a purpose for you.
You are not hopeless—
For God is your future.
You are not unaccepted, rejected, or abandoned—
For God loves you with an everlasting love.

How does God make His presence known to you?

My Prayer

*Thou, even Thou, art Lord alone; Thou hast made heaven,
the heaven of heavens, with all their host, the earth, and all things
that are therein, the seas, and all that is therein, and Thou
preservest them all; and the host of heaven worshippeth Thee.*

NEHEMIAH 9:6 KJV

Grace

God is full of grace. What a wonderful word grace is to us, what a wonderful gift it is in us, what a glorious provision it is for us.

Today, take a few moments and soak in the truth of His grace...

Are you receiving God's grace in your life today?

My Prayer

From the fullness of His grace we have all received one blessing after another.

JOHN 1:16 NIV

Grace Upon Grace

Gods' grace is poured upon you— the grace of His acceptance, the grace of His favor, the grace of pleasure, the grace of His liberty. Soak again today in more of God's amazing grace.

In what ways is God's grace amazing?

My Prayer

My grace is sufficient for thee: for my strength is made perfect in weakness. Most gladly therefore will I rather glory in my infirmities, that the power of Christ may rest upon me. 2 CORINTHIANS 12:9 KJV

You Can, Because He Can

You can ask of the Lord
because He will not give you a wrong answer.
You can wait upon the Lord
because His timing is always perfect.
You can trust in the Lord
because He makes no mistakes.
You can hope in the Lord
because He holds your future.
You can rest in the Lord
because He is in control of your life.
You can lean upon the Lord
because He is completely faithful.

What are you asking of God and do you believe that He will answer?

My Prayer

I know that You can do everything, and that
no purpose of Yours can be withheld from You.

JOB 42:2

His Easy Yoke

Beautiful in all Your splendor,
I yield to You in full surrender.
I turn from all that's not Your best,
And take my place within Your rest.
Strife and worry, all must cease,
When I'm abiding in Your peace.
I take Your yoke, there is no toil,
Lord, pour on me Your holy oil.

Are you taking ample time out to find rest in Him?

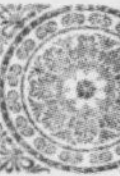

My Prayer

Come unto Me, all ye that labor and are heavy laden, and I will give you rest. Take My yoke upon you, and learn of Me; for I am meek and lowly in heart: and ye shall find rest unto your souls. For My yoke is easy, and My burden is light.

MATTHEW 11:28-30 KJV

Lord, Speak through Me

Lord, may the words I speak be a sweet sound in Your ear and a blessing to others. Speak through me the soothing words that will heal a hurting heart; the wise words that will guide a seeking heart; the assuring words that will comfort a grieving heart; the accepting words that will embrace a lonely heart; the affirming words that will strengthen a fearful heart; the life-giving words that will fill an empty heart.

How is the Holy Spirit speaking through you today?

My Prayer

A word fitly spoken is like apples of gold in settings of silver. PROVERBS 25:11

When You Need Him Most

His strongest grace
is for your weakest moment;
His sweetest fellowship
is for your loneliest journey;
His richest supply
is for your neediest hour;
His closest embrace
is for your deepest sorrow;
His brightest light
is for your darkest day.

When do you rely on God the most?

My Prayer

Can anything ever separate us from Christ's love? Does it mean He no longer loves us if we have trouble or calamity, or are persecuted, or hungry, or destitute, or in danger, or threatened with death?... No power in the sky above or in the earth below—indeed, nothing in all creation will ever be able to separate us from the love of God that is revealed in Christ Jesus our Lord. ROMANS 8:35, 39 NLT

Does God Love You?

Does God love you? Yes, Jesus died and rose for you.
Does God care about you? Yes, Jesus died and rose for you.
Will God save you and restore you? Yes, Jesus died and rose for you.
Will God provide for you? Yes, Jesus died and rose for you.

Do you recognize God's love and care for you today?

My Prayer

Much more then, having now been justified by His blood,
we shall be saved from wrath through Him. For if when we were enemies
we were reconciled to God through the death of His Son, much more,
having been reconciled, we shall be saved by His life.

ROMANS 5:9-10

All Is Yours

Does not justification, sanctification, redemption, and all the other truths of Scripture become yours because Jesus died and rose for you? The answer is yes. Yes, a million times over! Your life in Him is now an all encompassing "Yes" because Jesus died and rose for you. Today, hope is yours, life is yours, heaven is yours, blessings upon blessings are yours, because Jesus died and rose for you.

Where does your hope rest today?

My Prayer

For all things are yours: whether...the world or life or death, or things present or things to come—all are yours. And you are Christ's, and Christ is God's.

1 CORINTHIANS 3:21-23

New Life

When Jesus comes to live within us He brings brand-new life, like springtime to our hearts—the cold, dark places in us are replaced with His glorious light; the cold places with His warmth, the barren places with His fruitfulness.

What season is your life currently in and what defines God's glorious light in your life today?

My Prayer

Therefore, if anyone is in Christ, he is a new creation;
old things have passed away; behold, all things have become new.

2 CORINTHIANS 5:17

Forget the former things;
do not dwell on the past.
See, I am doing a new thing!
Now it springs up; do you not perceive it?
I am making a way in the desert
and streams in the wasteland.

ISAIAH 43:18–19 NIV

The Gift We Give To God

God's generosity to us in Jesus Christ is overwhelming—God gives us a clean heart, a joyful heart, a loving heart, a peaceful heart—yet, there is one thing God cannot give us, and that is a thankful heart. Thankfulness is our gift to Him.

How are you showing thankfulness to God today?

My Prayer

Then as He entered a certain village, there met Him ten men who were lepers, who stood afar off. And they lifted up their voices and said, "Jesus, Master, have mercy on us!"...And one of them, when he saw that he was healed, returned, and with a loud voice glorified God.

LUKE 17:12-13, 15

The Assurance of His Presence

The meaning of "Tabernacle" reaches into the deepest places of our hearts. Its impact was first known to the people of Israel in the book of Exodus (29:5), was revealed to the early church through the Gospels (JOHN 1:14), and is spoken of in the book of Revelation as an extension of God's loving care to His people in the final days (REVELATION 7:15). The word "Tabernacle" brings to us one of the clearest revelations of the love and care of God for His people. It says to us that God has chosen to come to us in our need, to draw close in intimacy and compassion, and to cover us with His presence.

How do I recognize the presence of God in my life?

My Prayer

And the Word (Christ) became flesh (human, incarnate) and tabernacled (fixed His tent of flesh, lived awhile) among us; and we [actually] saw His glory (His honor, His majesty), such glory as an only begotten son receives from his father, full of grace (favor, loving-kindness) and truth.

JOHN 1:14 AMP

The Comfort of His Presence

When God's people go through great hardships and heartaches we often wonder what can be said that will bring true comfort and hope. One of the things we can say with strong affirmation is that God is there, in the midst of it all, drawing closer than any friend or family member ever could. This is at the heart of Jesus, our Tabernacle. Jesus didn't stay away from us, hiding from our sorrows in heaven; He came to us and was among us.

Do you recognize God's comfort in your life or do you end up searching elsewhere for it?

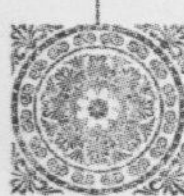

My Prayer

And I heard a loud voice from heaven saying, "Behold, the tabernacle of God is with men, and He will dwell with them, and they shall be His people. God Himself will be with them and be their God." REVELATION 21:3

God Is Close to You

The Bible tells us that God collects our tears in His bottle, and that one day He will wipe away all tears from our eyes. He is closer to you than anyone could ever be, and He does more for you than anyone could ever do. God is right beside you, every step of the way.

How do you face your greatest trials and difficulties?

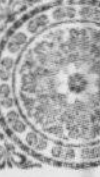

My Prayer

God will wipe away every tear from their eyes; there shall be no more death, nor sorrow, nor crying. There shall be no more pain, for the former things have passed away. REVELATION 21:4

There's No Place Like Home!

The saddest story of all is to learn of someone who is spiritually homeless. There is no greater emptiness, loneliness, or isolation than this. Jesus Christ came to make His home within our hearts. His presence makes it possible for every person to find their true home now and their eternal home with Him in heaven.

Are you wandering in your walk with the Lord or at home with Him?

My Prayer

If anyone loves Me, he will keep My word; and My Father will love him, and we will come to him and make our home with him.

JOHN 14:23

Work and Rest

Work is a good thing. Work is in the will of God. It is a way we honor and obey God. Work is a blessing. If we are out of work, we can ask God to lead us and to provide us with honorable work that will glorify Him.

Are you honoring God with your work or honoring your own efforts?

My Prayer

Six days you shall work, but on the seventh day you shall rest; in plowing time and in harvest you shall rest.

EXODUS 34:21

Will the "Real You" Please Stand Up!

If you do not know who you are in Christ, you will not be able to "stand up" to your true identity. Because you are in Christ, you cannot let the devil try to tag you with a false identity.

You are the Lord's person and possession. He made you and He owns you. He has ownership of you through creation and redemption. Isn't it good to know that you are doubly His! You are no small thing to Him and your life is no small matter in His loving hands.

Do you know who you are in Christ?

My Prayer

Fear not, for I have redeemed you;
I have called you by your name; you are Mine.

ISAIAH 43:1

Ministry

We don't have a ministry because we decide to have one; we have a ministry because God gives us one. Our calling, our work, and the fruit that comes from it is God's doing, not ours. Our privilege is to obey what God tells us to do; our responsibility is to serve Him faithfully in the place of obedience, whether it is a hidden place or a public place. His blessing and His anointing come to us when we are living in agreement with His will.

Are you seeking Him, running from Him or responding to His call today?

My Prayer

Paul, a bondservant of Jesus Christ, called to be an apostle, separated to the gospel of God.

ROMANS 1:1

What's Entering Your Thoughts

When a thought of anxiety comes knocking on the door of your mind, you must refuse it entrance. If you invite it in, it will have dinner with you, and if it has dinner with you it will quickly move in and want to spend the night.

What is controlling your thoughts...anxiety or anticipation of things to come from God?

My Prayer

The weapons of our warfare are not carnal but mighty in God for pulling down strongholds, casting down arguments and every high thing that exalts itself against the knowledge of God, bringing every thought into captivity to the obedience of Christ.

2 CORINTHIANS 10:4-5

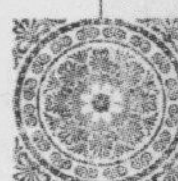

The Word of God

No one can put a chain around God's Word and limit its movement, bind its purpose, chain its influence, weaken its authority, or contain its power.
No warrior can dull the edges of its blade;
No intellectual can undermine its truth;
No skeptic can lessen its authenticity;
No mocker can weaken its foundations;
No philosopher can out-think its penetrating insight;
No strongman can weaken its power;
No religion can replace its transforming power.

The Word of God is powerful and true. Do you rely on it daily to strengthen your faith?

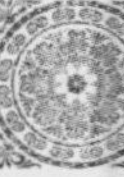

My Prayer

God's word is mighty in you today.
Let it be your guiding light.
HEBREWS 4:12 PARAPHRASED

How Does God Love You

God loves you:

With a love that reaches to the heights;
With a love that goes to the depths;
With a love that calls you, woos you,
draws you, keeps you, and
holds you close to His heart.

How will you show love to others today?

My Prayer

Christ will make His home in your hearts as you trust in Him. Your roots will grow down into God's love and keep you strong. And may you have the power to understand, as all God's people should, how wide, how long, how high, and how deep His love is. May you experience the love of Christ, though it is too great to understand fully. Then you will be made complete with all the fullness of life and power that comes from God.

EPHESIANS 3:17-19 NLT

The Future

Jesus is our future. He has called us to follow Him with a heart of faith and a life of obedience. In good times, in troubled times, or in uncertain times, all our times are in His hands. Our future is as bright as the promises of God; as hopeful as the faithfulness of God; as secure as the character of God; as abounding as the grace of God; as abundant as the love of God.

Is your heart set on following Him with your all?

My Prayer

Now all glory to God, who is able, through His mighty power at work within us, to accomplish infinitely more than we might ask or think. Glory to Him in the church and in Christ Jesus through all generations forever and ever! Amen.

EPHESIANS 3:20-21 NLT

Receiving and Waiting

In your walk with God two things will always be true: You will be receiving from Him and you will be waiting upon Him. Your faith must trust Him for both. You need to receive from Him what is yours for today and wait upon Him for what will be yours tomorrow.

Are you being patient and relying on your faith for what He has for you to receive?

What have you been waiting on from the Lord?

My Prayer

Wait patiently for the Lord. Be brave and courageous. Yes, wait patiently for the Lord.

PSALMS 27:14 NLT

Fret Busters

If you are heavy laden, come and receive Jesus' easy yoke; if you are stressed, come and receive Jesus' light burden; if you are weary, come and receive Jesus' rest. When you are yoked to Jesus you are not yoked to heaviness, drudgery, or despair. There is no Scripture that says, "If you enjoy what you are doing, you must be out of God's will."

How will you find release from your burden?

My Prayer

I delight to do Your will, O my God. PSALMS 40:8

You Can

You can believe God like Abraham because He is the same God;
You can praise Him like David because He is the same God;
You can worship Him like Isaiah because He is the same God;
You can cry out to Him like Moses because He is the same God;
You can serve Him like Ezra because He is the same God.

Do you believe the God of the Bible is the same God today?

My Prayer

I can do all things through Christ who strengthens me. PHILIPPIANS 4:13

Commit to the Lord whatever you do,
and your plans will succeed.

PROVERBS 16:3 NIV

Changeless

God never changes. He is perfect—without flaw, error, inconsistency, mistake, or poor judgment. God is not moody. He doesn't have good moods and bad moods. He is always righteous. His goodness, His purity, His holy nature, His justice, and His character are eternal.

How can you fully trust Him and obey Him today?

My Prayer

I am the Lord, I do not change. MALACHI 3:6 AMP

Not That Way

Our flesh doesn't mind doing things for God as long as it will make us look good or get us special recognition. God's ways are not our ways. Our faith must respond to what God wants us to do and how He wants us to do it, even if that way may seem inconvenient or take us out of our comfort zone.

Are you following what God wants you to do or pursuing your own wants?

My Prayer

Nevertheless not My will, but Yours, be done. LUKE 22:42

Not in This Place

When we say to God, "Yes, use me," that does not mean that our obedience of faith is complete. We must by faith add this commitment to our prayer, "Yes, Lord, use me now, in this moment." God wants to use us in His appointed time, not ours. We cannot live a life of faith and put things off for another day when God says, "Do it now."

Are you responding to what God wants from you today?

My Prayer

So I said, "Who are You, Lord?" And He said, "I am Jesus, whom you are persecuting. But rise and stand on your feet; for I have appeared to you for this purpose, to make you a minister and a witness both of the things which you have seen and of the things which I will yet reveal to you"... I was not disobedient to the heavenly vision. ACTS 26:15-16, 19

Not Me

There used to be a prayer of the uncommitted that said, "Here I am Lord, send my brother." When we say "not me" we place the focus upon ourselves, our limitations and weaknesses. However, faith says, "God can." Gideon told God, "I can't" but God told Gideon, "(You can) because I have sent you and I will be with you" (JUDGES 6:14-16).

Are you listening to the voice of the Holy Spirit today? What is He asking of you?

My Prayer

Also I heard the voice of the Lord, saying: "Whom shall I send,
And who will go for us?" Then I said, "Here am I! Send me."

ISAIAH 6:8

The Humble Place

God's grace works within our lives to strip us and reduce us, to mold us and shape us, to conform us into His image and to transform us into His likeness. God must reveal to us our true needs, and cause us to see how truly dependent we are upon Him. God does this, not to leave us empty, but to fill us with His true riches found in Jesus Christ.

Are you running on empty today? What can you do to depend on God today to fill you up?

My Prayer

For thus says the high and lofty One—He who inhabits eternity, whose name is Holy: I dwell in the high and holy place, but with him also who is of a thoroughly penitent and humble spirit, to revive the spirit of the humble and to revive the heart of the thoroughly penitent [bruised with sorrow for sin].

ISAIAH 57:15 AMP

Extending God's Opportunities

Each day we can respond to the opportunities God places before us. Not opportunities to be famous, powerful, or rich, but opportunities to glorify Him. These opportunities will often be found amidst the ordinary days, and routine moments of our lives. Today, God may give you the opportunity to perform an action that expresses what He wants to do in a certain situation; to share words that speak His heart and His truth into someone's life; to express kindness that extends His grace and mercy to someone in need.

How can you extend God's heart to another person?

My Prayer

We are God's masterpiece. He has created us anew in Christ Jesus,
so we can do the good things He planned for us long ago.

EPHESIANS 2:10 NLT

True Hope

No man or government has the power to change the greatest enemies that face every generation. It is foolish to put our hope in man. Man has no power to change the human heart, to deliver from sin, to take away the darkness that covers the soul, or to stop the certainty of death. When Jesus is your future you can set your heart, your thoughts, your faith, and your hope in Him because He cannot fail and He will never change.

Are you putting all your hope in Jesus today?

My Prayer

Paul, an apostle of Jesus Christ, by the commandment of God our Savior and the Lord Jesus Christ, our hope.

1 TIMOTHY 1:1

Hope in God's Eternal Plan

Jesus told those who would follow Him not to expect things to be easy; but this is not the time for those who know their God to be downcast or gloomy.

Are you rejoicing in the Lord today and in His eternal plan?

My Prayer

The world is passing away, and the lust of it;
but he who does the will of God abides forever.

1 JOHN 2:17

Keep Your Heart Full of Hope

Today, God wants us to keep our hope in Him and not in this world's system or its leaders. Jesus has kept us in the world but we are not of the world. He has us here for an eternal purpose—to be a light of hope that needs to be seen; to be a voice of truth that needs to be heard; to be a demonstration of love that needs to be lived.

How are you keeping your hope in God versus trying to search for hope through other sources?

My Prayer

The kingdoms of this world have become the kingdoms
of our Lord and of His Christ, and He shall reign forever and ever!
REVELATION 11:15

Your Value

Have you ever wondered what your true value is? If your life were up for auction what would you be worth? When Jesus went to the cross He paid the highest price that could ever be paid for your life. You are worth to God the death of His Son. Why such a high price? There are not 100 of you; there are not 10 of you; there is only one of you.

What value do you place on your life today?

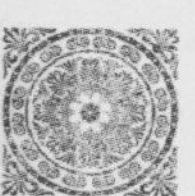

My Prayer

Christ died for us. ROMANS 5:8

Jesus Makes All the Difference

Live in the peace of knowing that God has accepted you.
Live in the confidence of knowing that Christ's blood makes you clean.
Live in the joy of knowing you are forgiven.
Live in the assurance of knowing that He is holding your hand.
Live in the hope of knowing that your future is secure with Jesus.

Reflect how Jesus is making a difference in your life.

My Prayer

Let it be known to you all, and to all the people of Israel, that by the name of Jesus Christ of Nazareth, whom you crucified, whom God raised from the dead, by Him this man stands here before you whole. This is the "stone which was rejected by you builders, which has become the chief cornerstone." Nor is there salvation in any other, for there is no other name under heaven given among men by which we must be saved.

ACTS 4:10-12

Jesus Is...

His majesty is your worship,
His holiness is your beauty,
His presence is your fragrance,
His truth is your foundation,
His tenderness is your comfort,
His abundance is your supply,
His plan is your purpose,
His faithfulness is your security,
His life is your fulfillment,
His strength is your endurance,
His heart is your home.

Is Jesus enough?

My Prayer

Because He is your Lord, worship Him. PSALMS 45:11

Looking Up; Looking Down

"Keep looking down!" This statement is a proclamation of a believer's position in Christ. Some think that the saying, "keep looking down" is a negative statement, while the phrase "keeping looking up" is a positive one. The truth is that both statements are positive when viewed from a proper perspective.

Are you seeing life from God's point of view?

My Prayer

He raised us from the dead along with Christ and seated us with Him in the heavenly realms because we are united with Christ Jesus.

EPHESIANS 2:6 NLT

Comfort

God's comfort is truly an amazing thing. Think about the image of a mother coming to the aid of her frightened child. The immediate response of the mother is to bring her child comfort. How does she do it? She brings comfort by reaching out and picking up her crying child in her arms.

Like that child, we all have need of God's comfort.
Have you felt His arms lift you and draw you close to His heart?
Have you heard His voice saying, "Peace, be still"?

My Prayer

All praise to God, the Father of our Lord Jesus Christ. God is our merciful Father and the source of all comfort. He comforts us in all our troubles.

2 CORINTHIANS 1:3-4 NLT

Abba Father

What is the loudest sound that you hear within you? What is the sound that rings the loudest day in and day out? Have you been quiet enough in your inner man to know? The loudest sounds that you hear and listen to are the true indicators of what is really happening in your spiritual walk. What you do and the choices you make are by-products of what is going on within you ~ Don Lessin

Is His voice the loudest sound in you?

My Prayer

You received the Spirit of adoption
by whom we cry out, "Abba, Father."
ROMANS 8:15

Whatever you do, whether in word or deed,
do it all in the name of the Lord Jesus,
giving thanks to God the Father through Him.

Colossians 3:17 NIV

The Heart of God Revealed

With gentle cords...God doesn't yank the cord He uses to draw us to Himself. He is patient with us. He waits for us to respond to His gentle tug upon our hearts. He does not attempt to overpower us—He comes to us meekly, peaceably and full of mercy.

What kind of response is God waiting on from you?

My Prayer

Now I, Paul, myself am pleading with you
by the meekness and gentleness of Christ.

2 CORINTHIANS 10:1

Jesus Is Coming Back

Jesus Christ is coming back. The outcome of all things has already been determined. Jesus is the winner. He is without rival in the universe. No evil doer, no outlaw, no terrorist, no anarchist will be standing in the end. Every enemy of God will be defeated, every false prophet will be exposed, every evil spirit will be chained, and every accusing tongue will be silenced.

The final chapter of history has already been written, and there will be no need for rewrites or revisions. God's plan will be fulfilled. There will be a new heaven and a new earth. One day soon, you will forever be with the Lord.

Are you living with eternity's values in view?

My Prayer

*For the Lord Himself shall descend from heaven with a shout,
with the voice of the archangel, and with the trump of God.*

1 THESSALONIANS 4:16 KJV

Blessed by the Blessed One

Rain is a blessing. Without it everything would die. The Bible tells us that God sends this blessing upon the just and the unjust. Believer and nonbeliever alike can experience and benefit from the blessings of God. His blessings bring sunshine and rain, seedtime and harvest, flowers and songbirds, and thousands of other things we experience throughout life by all who live upon the earth.

How are you blessed today?

My Prayer

The God and Father of our
Lord Jesus Christ, who is blessed forever.

2 CORINTHIANS 11:31

Real Grace

The life of Jesus brings us into reality, not role playing. In order to live in His reality we must first be real with Him. He wants us to come to Him as we are. He knows everything about us. We do not need to try and impress Him or win Him over with a good performance. We must come to Him in sincerity and truth, in humility and brokenness, and in openness and honesty. When we come to Him in this way, He will not cast us out. He does not meet us with judgment but with mercy; He does not extend condemnation but grace.

Are you being real and honest with God? He wants us to come to Him as we are.

My Prayer

The grace of our Lord Jesus Christ be with you all. 2 THESSALONIANS 3:18

The Reality of His Grace

"All the world's a stage, and all the men and women merely players." For many people, life is nothing more than playing out a role. They "act" their way through life, trying to gain the approval and acceptance of others. They are bound by the fear of being exposed for who they really are, and so they perform, playing out a role in order to receive applause and recognition. Many Christians live this way, trying to impress others by acting out a spiritual role.

God has not called us to role playing, but to reality living based upon His grace. There's no point in "acting" like everything is great, instead, go to God in prayer and receive His grace.

How are you approaching your life—reality or role playing?

My Prayer

The law was given through Moses;
grace and truth came through Jesus Christ.

JOHN 1:17 NIV

Receiving His Grace

Grace is one of the most freeing things we can ever receive and experience in life. Grace justifies you and brings you His salvation (TITUS 2:11, 3:7.) Grace means that God has accepted you and received you into His family as His child, not because of your good performance, but because of what Jesus Christ has done for you. Grace means that God freely gives you what you don't deserve. Today draw near to God and receive His grace.

Do you freely receive God's grace?

My Prayer

He gives more grace. Therefore He says: "God resists the proud, but gives grace to the humble." Therefore submit to God. Resist the devil and he will flee from you. Draw near to God and He will draw near to you. JAMES 4:6-8

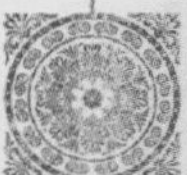

Come into His Grace

Do you sense your weakness? There's no need to grit your teeth and bear it with a painted smile, instead accept the strength that God gives you through His grace.

How are you drawing upon the comfort and hope that comes to you through His grace?

My Prayer

Let us therefore come boldly to the throne of grace, that we may obtain mercy and find grace to help in time of need.

HEBREWS 4:16

Walk in His Grace

Do you want to live a life that is pleasing to God? There's no need to strive and try to make things happen, instead, walk in the grace that enables you to glorify Him.

How will you glorify the Lord today and walk in His grace?

My Prayer

Now may our Lord Jesus Christ Himself and God our Father, who loved us and by His grace gave us eternal comfort and a wonderful hope, comfort you and strengthen you in every good thing you do and say. 2 THESSALONIANS 2:16-17 NLT

Waiting

God doesn't always answer our prayers at the moment we ask. It may be His plan to answer us, but not always in the timetable we think. Also, God doesn't always fulfill the words He speaks to us at the moment He reveals them.

Why does God sometimes delay and what does He want us to learn while we are waiting?

My Prayer

We desire that each one of you show the same diligence to the full assurance of hope until the end, that you do not become sluggish, but imitate those who through faith and patience inherit the promises. HEBREWS 6:11-12

Jesus Our Only Option

Our decision to know and follow God is so important that He has presented us with only one option. Every road sign God has made points to one person; every message God has spoken proclaims one name; every view God shows us of Himself reveals one face. This moment, for you, Jesus Christ is God's only option.

How will you proclaim Jesus as the only option in your life?

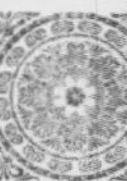

My Prayer

Yet for us there is one God, the Father, of whom are all things, and we for Him; and one Lord Jesus Christ, through whom are all things, and through whom we live. 1 CORINTHIANS 8:6

Jesus as Your Plan A

Jesus is God's Plan A. Because Plan A is perfect and complete, there is no need for a Plan B. God has no backup plan for your life. He doesn't need one. God never says to us, "If Jesus, My Son, doesn't work for you, let's try something else." Any Plan B is our plan, which comes from our own thinking and rationale. God tells us not to lean upon our own understanding, but to acknowledge Him, the Lord in every decision and the director of our steps.

How is Jesus your Plan A?

My Prayer

Troubles nearly always make us look to God; His blessings are apt to make us look elsewhere. Narrow all your interests until the attitude of mind and heart and body is concentration on Jesus Christ. – OSWALD CHAMBERS

Clean Hands and a Pure Heart

If God has called you to serve Him, you must do so with clean hands and a pure heart. God never tells us to walk righteously before Him and live unrighteous before others; He never tells us to be excellent in our work or service and have a mediocre relationship with Him. Who we are before Him and how we are before others are both important to God.

Are you prepared to serve God today?

Are you coming to Him with clean hands and a pure heart?

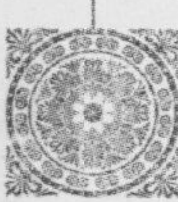

My Prayer

Now may the God of peace who brought up our Lord Jesus from the dead, that great Shepherd of the sheep, through the blood of the everlasting covenant, make you complete in every good work to do His will, working in you what is well pleasing in His sight, through Jesus Christ, to whom be glory forever and ever. Amen. HEBREWS 13:20-21

Set Apart

You have been set apart for fellowship, for relationship, and for companionship. You have been set apart to be edified, encouraged, and to grow up in the knowledge of the Lord. You are His sanctified vessel—with a high and holy calling, with an eternal hope and purpose, with a Divine commission to make Him known, and with an inheritance that is beyond the reach of decay, unfading, reserved in heaven for you.

Do you have a hope and a purpose that is aligned with God's high and holy calling on your life?

My Prayer

So use your whole body as an instrument
to do what is right for the glory of God.

ROMANS 6:13 NLT

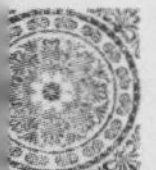

Assurance

May Jesus assure you that as you follow Him—you will never meet a fear He cannot conquer; you will never face an enemy He cannot defeat; you will never enter a battle He cannot win; you will never have a need He cannot meet; you will never face a temptation He cannot overcome; you will never have a burden He cannot lift; you will never face a problem He cannot solve; you will never have a bondage He cannot break; you will never have a moment when He does not care; you will never have a time when He is not there.

Where does your assurance rest today—in your ability or in God's?

My Prayer

I have strength for all things in Christ who empowers me [I am ready for anything and equal to anything through Him who infuses inner strength into me; I am self-sufficient in Christ's sufficiency]. PHILIPPIANS 4:13 AMP

Jesus Will Never Let You Go

His hands that hold you are pierced hands. If you ever question His love for you, look at His hands. His arms were once outstretched on the cross so that He could embrace you now with His unfailing love.

Today your life couldn't be in better hands.

My Prayer

[For it is He] who rescued and saved us from such a perilous death, and He will still rescue and save us; in and on Him we have set our hope (our joyful and confident expectation) that He will again deliver us [from danger and destruction and draw us to Himself].

2 CORINTHIANS 1:10 AMP

The Lord your God is with you,
He is mighty to save.
He will take great delight in you,
He will quiet you with His love,
He will rejoice over you with singing.
ZEPHANIAH 3:17 NIV

In God We Trust

We can trust in God because—

His kingdom is unshakable.
His throne is incorruptible.
His glory is indescribable.
His Word is infallible.
His greatness is unsearchable.
His power is invincible.
His favor is invaluable.
His grace is inexpressible.
His love is undeniable.

Are you putting total trust in the Lord?

How can you strengthen your trust in Him today?

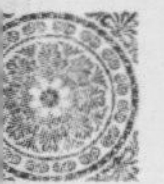

My Prayer

It is good for me to draw near to God;
I have put my trust in the Lord God.

PSALMS 73:28

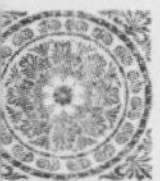
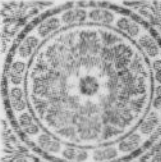

Fullness of Joy

It is as though God is saying to us, "The joys that come from the blessings I give you can only go so far, for they are *from Me,* but they are not *Me*. I want you to enjoy what I give you, but even more, I want you to have Me—My life, My love, My presence. It is with Me, in Me, and from Me alone that you will know the fullness of joy I want you to have."

How are you experiencing God's fullness of joy in your life today?

My Prayer

You will show me the path of life; in Your presence is fullness of joy, at Your right hand there are pleasures forevermore.

PSALMS 16:11

Untangled Knots

How are we to respond to problems we cannot solve, to conflicts we cannot settle, to differences we cannot reconcile, to difficulties we cannot fix, to complications we cannot sort out, to heartaches we cannot heal, to tensions we cannot ease? The answer is not to struggle, to strive, or to become perplexed trying to work things out in our own wisdom and strength. These are the times when we need to remain hopeful, to renew our trust in the Lord, and to place things in His skilled hands. Only He can heal what we cannot mend, reconcile what we cannot restore, and straighten what we cannot untie.

Are you relying on God or trying to solve life's issues on your own?

My Prayer

Every valley shall be lifted and filled up, and every mountain and hill shall be made low; and the crooked and uneven shall be made straight and level, and the rough places a plain. ISAIAH 40:4 AMP

God Is

For every hectic day, God is your quiet rest.
For every painful experience, God is your healing touch.
For every disappointment, God is your certain hope.
For every turbulent storm, God is your calming peace.
For every hurtful action, God is your forgiving love.

What is God for you today?

My Prayer

Happy (blessed, fortunate, enviable) is he who has the God of [special revelation to] Jacob for his help, whose hope is in the Lord his God.

PSALMS 146:5 AMP

Road Noise

Is the pace of your life creating a high level of "road noise?" Is the sound of His still small voice barely discernable? If so, it is time to quiet your heart. It is time to "Be still and know that He is God." It is time to wait upon the Lord and have your strength renewed. It is time to hear Him say to you, "Peace, be still!"

Are you being patient, listening, and waiting upon the Lord?

How do you "be still" and know that "He is God" in your life?

My Prayer

I will hear what God the Lord will speak,
for He will speak peace to His people.
PSALMS 85:8

I Am With You Always

I am near! Don't doubt My presence for a single moment. I am the true and faithful God. Be as certain of Me fulfilling My promise as I was when I first spoke it. Don't doubt it. Let your heart be quiet with this assurance! I am with you because I care about you. I am with you because I love you. I am with you because I want to be with you. I am with you because I desire to have fellowship with you. There will never be a time, a moment, a second when you are without Me. I am with you now. With you tomorrow. With you in the dark times. With you in the hard times. With you in the glad times. With you through all the times of your life.

What can you do today to live your life as "one" with Him?

My Prayer

It is fine to be zealous, provided the purpose is good,
and to be so always, not just when I am with you.
GALATIANS 4:18 NIV

Walking in the Spirit

To walk in the spirit means the manner in which we live our lives as we allow the Holy Spirit to conform us to the image of Jesus Christ. Walking in the Spirit means an active life, one that is responsive to the Holy Spirit's work, rather than a passive life, which does not respond. Walking in the Spirit means going at His pace and not our own pace. Sometimes we want to force fruit to grow, or hurry and pick fruit that is not ready to be harvested. Walking in the Spirit also means following His direction and not blazing our own trails.

Are you listening to Him and walking in His direction?

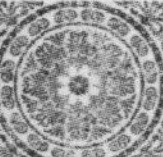

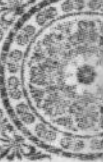

My Prayer

If we live in the Spirit, let us also walk in the Spirit. GALATIANS 5:25

You Are the Lord's

You are the Lord's and He has the final say. You are the Lord's and He is the final authority. No scheme of the enemy and no plan of man need take from you what Jesus came to give to you and to be to you.

Do you claim Him as Lord today?

My Prayer

The thief does not come except to steal, and to kill, and to destroy. I have come that they may have life, and that they may have it more abundantly.

JOHN 10:10

If

If Jesus is who He says He is,
If Jesus can do all He said He can do,
If Jesus can be all He has promised to be,
If Jesus will come like He said He would come,
If Jesus loves you like He said He loves you,

You have no reason to worry or fear, and every reason to be at rest.

Jesus gives you the assurance needed to live your life in confidence and rest (in Him). Do you question things in your life that are creating unrest for you?

My Prayer

Peace I leave with you, My peace I give to you; not as the world gives do I give to you. Let not your heart be troubled, neither let it be afraid.

JOHN 14:27

When You Sense Him Most

It is often in the hardest place that you hear God's softest voice; in the weakest moment that you find His greatest strength; in the loneliest hour that you sense His closest companionship; in the deepest sorrow that you feel His gentlest touch; in the darkest time that you see His brightest light; in the fiercest trial that you find His fullest peace; in the harshest rejection that you know His warmest embrace.

Do you draw close to God when you sense the need for comfort in your life?

My Prayer

Blessed be the God and Father of our Lord Jesus Christ, the Father of sympathy (pity and mercy) and the God [who is the Source] of every comfort (consolation and encouragement), who comforts (consoles and encourages) us in every trouble (calamity and affliction).

2 CORINTHIANS 1:3-4 AMP

Continue

Continue in the things that concern Him;
He will continue to take care of the things that concern you.
Continue to give Him all that is yours;
He will continue to give you all that is His.
Continue to wait upon Him;
He will continue to be faithful to you.
Continue to seek His best;
He will continue to give you His highest.

How will you continue to respond to God's best in your life?

My Prayer

Obey Me, and I will be your God, and you will be
My people. Do everything as I say, and all will be well!

JEREMIAH 7:23 NLT

In His Hands

The best decision you ever made was to place your life into the hands of the One who made you—hands that work with SKILL; hands that guide with WISDOM; hands that shape with PURPOSE; hands that form with LOVE.

What guides your thoughts, shapes your purpose, and forms your love?

My Prayer

For You, O Lord, have made me glad by Your works;
at the deeds of Your hands I joyfully sing.

PSALMS 92:4 AMP

Commit to the Lord whatever you do,
and your plans will succeed.

Proverbs 16:3 NIV

Notes

ROY LESSIN

MEET ME in the MEADOW

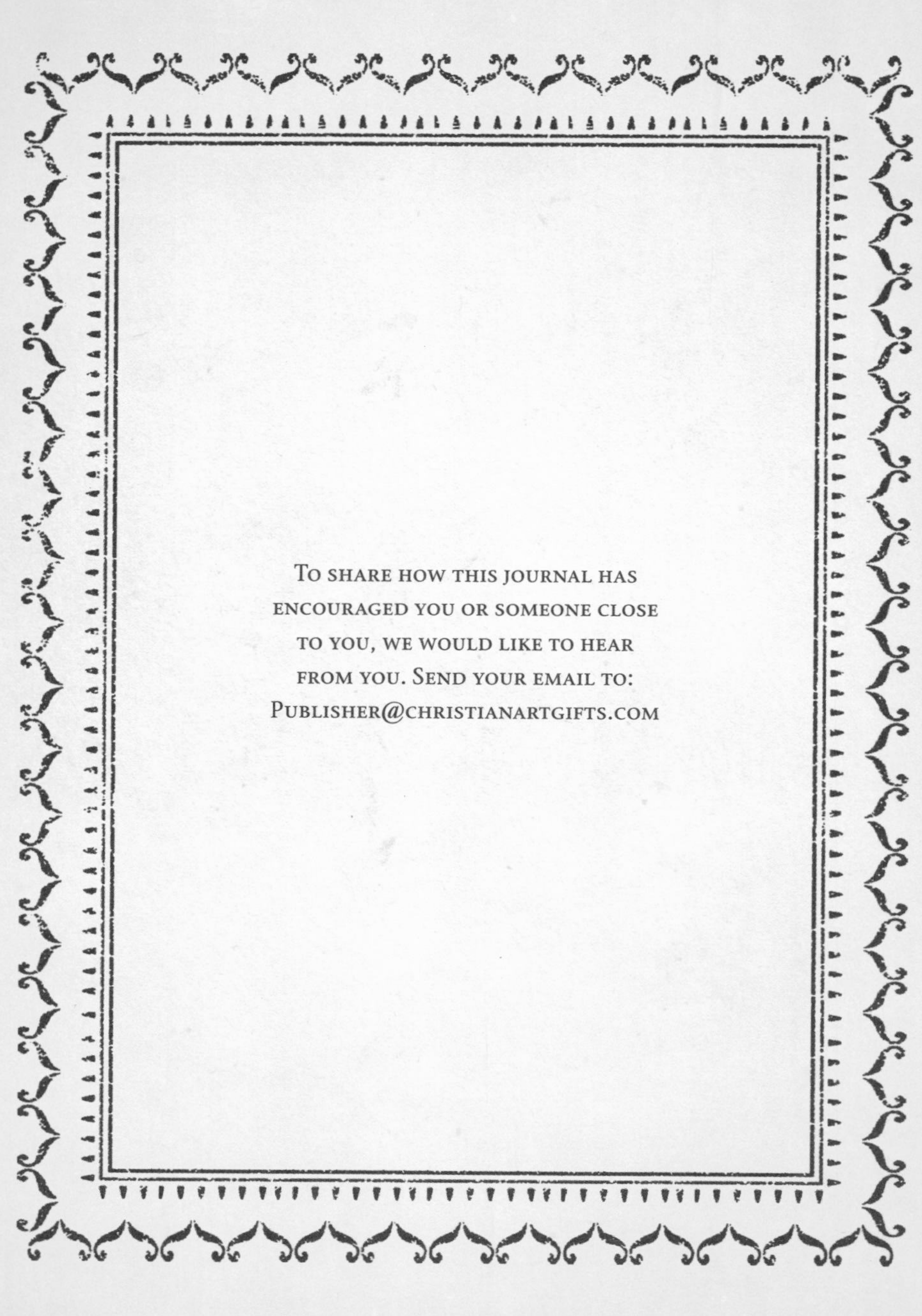

To share how this journal has encouraged you or someone close to you, we would like to hear from you. Send your email to:
Publisher@christianartgifts.com